MY FIRST EVERYDAY WORDS IN CANTONESE & ENGLISH

日常粵/英語初學

BY KAREN YEE

FOR VER

For a free audio recording and other books visit:
www.greencowsbooks.com

(c) 2017, Karen Yee
Green Cows Books
Inquiries: everydaycantonese@gmail.com

ISBN: 978-0999273036

早晨! 我...

zou2 san4! ngo5 ...

(jo sun! ngo ...)

Good Morning!
I ...

醒
seng2
(sang)

wake up

洗頭髮
sai2 tau4 faat3
(sigh tuw faht)

wash
my hair

飲奶
jam2 naai5
(yem nigh)

drink milk

我著 ...

ngo5 zoek3 ...

(ngo jerk ...)

I put on my...

衫
saam1
(sahm)

shirt

襪
mut6
(mutt)

socks

褲
fu3
(foo)

pants

衫裙
saam1 kwan4
(sahm kwun)

dress

鞋
haai4
(high)

shoes

褸
lau1
(luw)

jacket

短褲
dyun2 fu3
(duen foo)

shorts

我 ...
ngo5 ...
(ngo ...)

I ...

行路
haang4 lou6
(hahng low)

walk

企起身
kei5 hei2 san1
(kay hay sun)

stand up

坐低
co5 dai1
(chuo dye)

sit down

爬
paa4
(pah)

crawl

踎低
mau1 dai1
(muw dye)

squat

游水
jau4 seoi2
(yuw seoi)

swim

跑步
paau2 bou6
(pow boh)

run

我鍾意 ...

ngo5 zung1 ji3 ...

(ngo joe(ng) yee ...)

I like to ...

玩
waan2
(wahn)

play

油油
jau4 jau2
(yuw yuw)

paint

讀書
duk6 syu1
(dook shoe)

read books

拖手
to1 sau2
(tuoh suw)

hold hands

行樓梯
haang4 lau4 tai1
(hahng luw tie)

walk on stairs

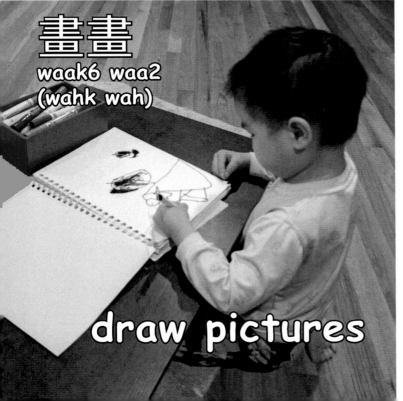

畫畫
waak6 waa2
(wahk wah)

draw pictures

微笑
mei4 siu3
(may siew)

smile

你想食乜野?
nei5 soeng2 sik6 mat1 je5?
(nay serng sik mutt yeh?)

What do you
want to eat?

香蕉
hoeng1 ziu1
(herng jew)

banana

蘋果
ping4 gwo2
(ping guo)

apple

橙
caang2
(chahng)

orange

士多啤梨
si6 do1 be1 lei2
(see dah beh lay)

strawberry

菠蘿
bo1 lo4
(buoh luoh)

pineapple

牛油果
ngau4 jau4 gwo2
(nguw yuw guo)

avocado

臉柿
nam4 ci2
(num chee)

persimmon

荔枝
lai6 zi1
(lye jee)

lychee

西瓜
sai1 gwaa1
(sigh gwah)

watermelon

葡提子
pou4 tai4 zi2
(poh tie jee)

grapes

木瓜
muk6 gwaa1
(muuk gwah)

papaya

我想食...
ngo5 soeng2 sik6 ...
(ngo serng sik ...)

I want to eat...

粟米
suk1 mai5
(suuk my)

corn

番茄
faan1 ke2
(fahn keah)

tomato

紅蘿蔔
hung4 lo4 baak6
(hoe(ng) luo bahk)

carrot

意大利瓜
ji3 daai6 lei6 gwaa1
(ee dah lay gwah)

zucchini squash

西蘭花
sai1 laan4 faa1
(sigh lahn fa)

broccoli

番薯
faan1 syu2
(fahn shoe)

sweet potato

椰菜花
je4 coi3 faa1
(yeh choy fa)

cauliflower

麵包
min6 baau1
(meen bao)

bread

飯
faan6
(fahn)

rice

蛋
daan6
(dahn)

egg

麵
min6
(meen)

noodles

我飲 ...
ngo5 jam2 ...
(ngo yem ...)

I drink ...

水
seoi2
(sui)

water

橙汁
caang2 zap1
(chahng jup)

orange juice

牛奶
ngau4 naai5
(nguw nigh)

milk

你想玩乜野?
nei5 soeng2 waan2 mat1 je5?
(nay serng wahn mutt yeh?)

What do you want to play?

火車
fo2 ce1
(fuoh chieh)

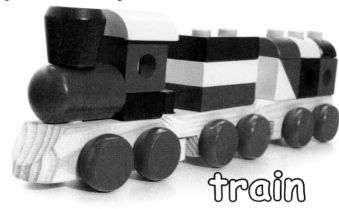

train

波
bo1
(buoh)

ball

車
ce1
(chieh)

car

砌圖
cai3 tou4
(chai toe)

puzzle

飛機
fei1 gei1
(fay gay)

airplane

三輪車
saam1 leon4 ce1
(sahm luon chieh)

tricycle

粉筆
fan2 bat1
(fun but)

chalk

我 ...
ngo5 ...
(ngo ...)

I ...

刷牙
caat3 ngaa4
(chaht nga)

brush my teeth

沖涼
cung1 loeng4
(cho(ng) lerng)

take a bath

換衫
wun6 saam1
(woon sahm)

change my clothes

早啲! 我瞓覺.

zou2 tau2! ngo5 fan3 gaau3.
(jo tuw! ngo fun gau.)

Good Night! I'm going to sleep.

點心
dim2 sam1
(deem sum)

dim sum

潮州粉果
ciu4 zau1 fan2 gwo2
(chew juw fun guo)

chew-juw
dumpling

蘿蔔糕
lo4 baak6 gou1
(luo bahk go)

turnip cake

生煎包
saang1 zin1 baau1
(sahng jeen bao)

pan-fried
pork bun

鍋貼
wo1 tip3
(wuo teep)

pan-fried
dumpling

鹹水角
haam4 seoi2 gok2
(hahm sui gok)
glutinous rice dumpling

叉燒包
caa1 siu1 baau1
(cha siu bao)
barbecue pork bun

芋角
wu6 gok2
(woo gok)
fried taro dumpling

鮮竹卷
sin1 zuk1 gyun2
(seen jook guun)
steamed tofu skin roll

蛋撻
daan6 taat1
(dahn taht)

egg
custard tart

煎堆
zin1 deoi1
(jean dui)

deep fried
sesame ball

蝦餃
haa1 gaau2
(ha gao)

shrimp dumpling

燒賣
siu1 maai2
(siu my)

shrimp &
pork dumpling

小籠包
siu2 lung4 baau1
(siew luong bao)

soup dumpling

韭菜餃
gau2 coi3 gaau2
(guw choy gao)

chives dumpling

蝦腸粉
haa1 coeng2 fan2
(ha cherng fun)

**shrimp
rice noodle**

粽
zung2
(joe(ng))

**sticky rice
dumpling**

芝麻湯圓
zi1 maa4 tong1 jyun2
(jee ma tong yuen)

glutinous rice ball
with sesame paste

芝麻糊
zi1 maa4 wu2
(jee ma woo)

black
sesame soup

奶黃包
naai5 wong4 baau1
(nai huang bao)

egg custard bun

杏仁豆腐
hang6 jan4 dau6 fu6
(hung yen duw foo)

almond tofu

GLOSSARY - DIM SUM
Each food is listed with Jyutping pronunciation and with simplified phonetic English.

(點心) **Dim Sum** (dim2 sam1 / deem sum) - Chinese cuisine of small, bite-sized portions of food, traditionally served with tea, for brunch.

(杏仁豆腐) **Almond tofu** (hang6 jan4 dau6 fu6 / hung yen duw foo) - soft jelly dessert made of almond, jelly and sugar. Tofu made of soybeans is not actually used.

(叉燒包) **Barbecue pork bun** (caa1 siu1 baau1 / cha siu bao) - savory bun filled with Chinese barbecue pork (char siu). Typically steamed, but can also be baked.

(芝麻糊) **Black sesame soup** (zi1 maa4 wu2 / jee ma woo)- dessert made of toasted black sesame, rice, sugar and water.

(潮州粉果) **Chew-Juw dumpling** (ciu4 zau1 fan2 gwo2 / chew juw fun guo) - steamed dumpling filled with ground pork, chopped peanuts, chives, dried shrimp, shiitake mushrooms and cilantro. The wrapping is extra thick.

(韭菜餃) **Chives dumpling** (gau2 coi3 gaau2 / guw choy gao) - dumpling filled with chives, pork and shrimp. It is often steamed and then pan-fried.

(煎堆) **Deep-fried sesame ball** (zin1 deoi1 / jean dui) - fried pastry made with glutinous rice flour and filled with red bean, lotus or black bean paste. Covered with sesame seeds.

(奶黃包) **Egg custard bun** (naai5 wong4 baau1 / nai huang bao) - sweet bun filled with egg custard. Typically steamed, but can also be baked.

(蛋撻) **Egg custard tart** (daan6 taat1 / dahn taht) - a pastry crust filled with egg custard, then baked.

(芋角) **Fried taro dumpling** (wu6 gok2 / woo gok) - deep-fried dumpling filled with pork, shrimp, garlic and green onions. The dumpling "skin" is made of steamed and mashed taro.

(芝麻湯圓) **Glutinous rice ball with sesame paste** (zi1 maa4 tong1 jyun2 / jee ma tong yuen) - dessert made of a glutinous rice dough, then filled with black sesame paste.

(鹹水角) **Glutinous rice dumpling** (haam4 seoi2 gok2 / hahm sui gok) - deep-fried dumpling filled with pork or chicken, shiitake mushrooms, carrots, water chestnuts and onion. The dumpling skin is made of glutinous rice flour.

(鍋貼) **Pan-fried dumpling** (wo1 tip3 / wuo teep) - pan-fried dumpling filled with pork or beef.

(生煎包) **Pan-fried pork bun** (saang1 zin1 baau1 / sahng jeen bough) - pan-fried steamed bun filled with pork and soup.

(燒賣) **Shrimp and pork dumpling** (siu1 maai2 / siu my) - steamed dumpling filled with pork and shrimp.

(蝦餃) **Shrimp dumpling** (haa1 gaau2 / ha gao) - steamed dumpling filled with shrimp.

(蝦腸粉) **Shrimp rice noodle** (haa1 coeng2 fan2 / ha cherng fun) - large flat noodle made of rice and wrapped around shrimp (or beef or barbecue pork) and steamed. Drizzled with soy sauce before eaten.

(小籠包) **Soup dumpling** (siu2 lung4 baau1 / siew luong bao) - steamed dumpling filled with pork and shrimp in a soup broth. The soup is made of a gelatin that melts into liquid when the bun is cooked.

(鮮竹卷) **Steamed tofu skin roll** (sin1 zuk1 gyun2 / seen jook guun) - beancurd skin wrapped around a filling of pork or chicken, water chestnuts and green onions, and then steamed.

(粽) **Sticky rice dumpling** (zung2 / joe(ng)) - glutinous rice flavored with chicken, shiitake mushrooms, Chinese sausage, pork belly, dried shrimp and salted egg yolk. It is wrapped in bamboo or other large leaves, then steamed.

(蘿蔔糕) **Turnip cake** (lo4 baak6 gou1 / luo bahk go) - savory cake made of daikon (white turnip) and rice flour, which typically also includes shrimp, pork and mushrooms. Typically pan-fried but can also be steamed.

NOTES

REMEMBERING CANTONESE TONES

Each Jyutping includes the tone (example: 貓 maau1 = tone 1). The six tones can be remembered using a mnemonic. To remember the Cantonese tones in order, speak the numbers "394052" (saam1 gau2 sei3 ling4 ng5 ji6) in Cantonese.

TONE	NUMBER	JYUTPING	ALTERNATE PHONETICS
Tone 1	"3"	saam1	sahm
Tone 2	"9"	gau2	guw
Tone 3	"4"	sei3	say
Tone 4	"0"	ling4	ling
Tone 5	"5"	ng5	mm
Tone 6	"2"	ji6	yee

ALTERNATE PRONUNCIATIONS

For words with more than one common pronunciation, this book tries to select the pronunciation that would be most easily understood when spoken by less fluent Cantonese speakers. For example, for 你(you): both "lei5 (lay)" and "nei5 (nay)" are common pronunciations. This book uses "nei (nay)", since less fluent Cantonese speakers may find they are more easily understood.

ABOUT THE AUTHOR

Karen Yee graduated from Stanford University and the Wharton School of Business, and was a National Spelling Bee finalist. She was inspired to create Cantonese bilingual books and the Cantonese for Kids series to help her own family have fun learning languages.

Made in the USA
Coppell, TX
14 December 2021

68544829R00019